FIGURING OUT GEOMETRY

MATH BUSTERS

Rebecca Wingard-Nelson

NEED MORE PRACTICE?
Free worksheets available at
http://www.enslow.com

Enslow Publishers, Inc.
40 Industrial Road
Box 398
Berkeley Heights, NJ 07922
USA

http://www.enslow.com

5/09   23 ^{00}

Library of Congress Cataloging-in-Publication Data

Wingard-Nelson, Rebecca.
Figuring out geometry / Rebecca Wingard-Nelson.
      p. cm. — (Math busters series)
Summary: "Presents a step-by-step guide to understanding geometry"—Provided by publisher.
    Includes bibliographical references and index.
    ISBN-13: 978-0-7660-2880-7
    ISBN-10: 0-7660-2880-1
  1. Geometry—Juvenile literature. I. Title.
    QA445.5.W554 2008
  516—dc22

                                            2007029383

Printed in the United States of America

10 9 8 7 6 5 4 3 2

To Our Readers: We have done our best to make sure all Internet Addresses in this book were active and appropriate when we went to press. However, the author and the publisher have no control over and assume no liability for the material available on those Internet sites or on other Web sites they may link to. Any comments or suggestions can be sent by e-mail to comments@enslow.com or to the address on the back cover.

Illustration credits: © 2007 Jupiterimages Corporation, pp. 8, 9, 19, 25, 29, 30, 32, 34, 38, 43, 48, 53, 55, 60, 61.

Cover photo: © 2007 Jupiterimages Corporation

Free Worksheets are available for this book at http://www.enslow.com. Search for the **Math Busters** series name. The publisher will provide access to the worksheets for five years from the book's first publication date.

Contents

Introduction

Not every person is an accountant,
engineer, rocket scientist, or math teacher.
However, every person does use math.

Most people never think, "I just used math to decide if I have
enough milk for this week!" But that is exactly what they did.
Math is everywhere; we just don't see it because it doesn't
always look like the math we do at school.

Math gives you the power to:
• determine the best route on a trip
• keep score in a game
• compare prices
• figure how much paint to buy
• plan a vacation schedule

Geometry is a kind of math that everyone uses.
It is used to give directions, like "turn left."
Geometry is used to play sports and games.
It is used to create structures like bridges and buildings.
Geometry is used in computer graphics, images,
and designs for art, media, and medicine.

This book will help you understand geometry.
It can be read from beginning to end,
or used to review a specific topic.

① Points, Lines, and Planes

Some geometric terms are words you use every day, but they have special meanings in geometry.

Points

In geometry, a **point** is an exact location in space.
The symbol for a point is a dot (•).
A point is usually named using a capital letter, like A, Q, or X.
A point can be written as Å, or point A.

Using Points

Points are used to name an exact location.

The blue dot is at point A.

The lines cross at Ż.

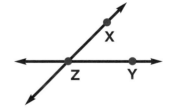

Lines

In geometry, a **line** is a straight set of points that extends in two directions and does not end. Arrows are used to show that a figure is a line.

The symbol for a line has arrows on each end (⟷).
Lines can be named by two points on the line: $\overleftrightarrow{AB}$, or line AB.
Lines can also be given a single letter name, like line d.

Horizontal, Vertical, and Oblique

$\overleftrightarrow{EF}$ is called a **horizontal** line.
It appears to go straight left and right.

$\overleftrightarrow{GH}$ is called a **vertical** line.
It appears to go straight up and down.

Line k is called an **oblique** line.
It is not horizontal or vertical.

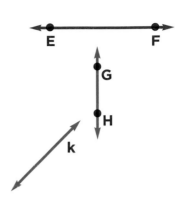

Planes

A **plane** is a flat surface that continues in all directions. You can think of a plane as a blackboard, a tabletop, or a floor that goes on in all directions forever.

Naming a Plane

Planes are named using any three points that lie on the plane. The plane below can be named plane LMN, MNL, LNM, or any other combination of the three points.

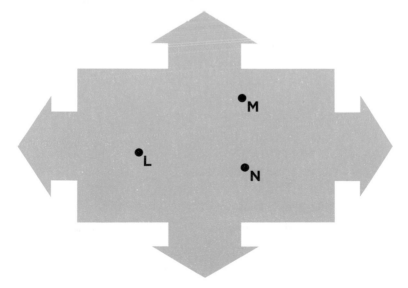

7

② Rays and Line Segments

Sometimes you only have part of a line. Part of a line is called either a ray or a line segment.

Rays

A **ray** is part of a line that starts at a point and extends forever in one direction.
The symbol for a ray has an arrow on one end (—→).
The point where the ray starts is called its **endpoint.**

Naming Rays

Name two rays in the figure below.

Step 1: The ray shown in red begins at point L and extends through point N. A ray is named using the endpoint first, then any other point on the ray.
The ray shown in red is named $\overrightarrow{LN}$.

Step 2: A ray can be part of a whole line in a figure. Use a point on the line as an endpoint. Use another point on the line to show in which direction the ray extends. You can use point L to name a ray that is part of $\overleftrightarrow{KM}$.
The ray shown in blue is named $\overrightarrow{LM}$.

Two rays in the figure are $\overrightarrow{LN}$ and $\overrightarrow{LM}$.

8

Line Segments

A **segment**, or **line segment**, is part of a line. It has two endpoints. A line segment is named using its endpoints. The symbol for a segment has no arrows (——).

Naming Line Segments

Name two line segments in the figure.

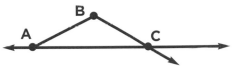

Step 1: Line segments are named using two endpoints in any order. The line segment shown in red has endpoints at point A and point B. The line segment shown in red can be named $\overline{AB}$ or $\overline{BA}$.

Step 2: A line segment can be part of a whole line or part of a ray in a figure. The line segment in blue is part of $\overrightarrow{BC}$. It can be named $\overline{BC}$ or $\overline{CB}$.

Two line segments in the figure are $\overline{AB}$ and $\overline{BC}$.

Manta rays and stingrays look like geometric **rays**. They have a straight tail, and a body that is shaped like an arrow. A segment on a worm is just one section, or piece, of the worm— just like a **line segment** is a piece of a line.

③ Line Relationships

When two or more lines are
in a figure, there are special terms that
tell how the lines are related.

Intersecting and Perpendicular Lines

Lines, rays, and line segments that meet are called **intersecting**.

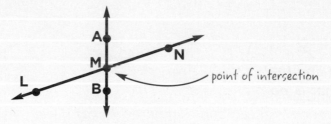

Line AB and line LN are intersecting lines.
Segment AB and segment LN are intersecting segments.
The point where the lines or segments meet, point M, is called
the **point of intersection.**

Perpendicular lines are intersecting lines that form four
right angles. Right angles measure exactly 90 degrees.

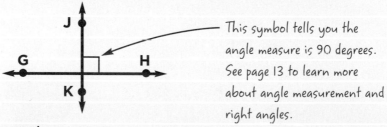

This symbol tells you the
angle measure is 90 degrees.
See page 13 to learn more
about angle measurement and
right angles.

The symbol $\perp$ means "is perpendicular to."
Line GH and line JK are perpendicular.
You can write this as $\overleftrightarrow{GH} \perp \overleftrightarrow{JK}$.

Parallel Lines

Parallel lines are in the same plane and never cross because they are always the same distance apart.
Segments and rays of parallel lines are also parallel.

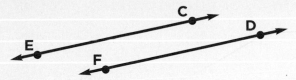

The symbol ‖ means "is parallel to."
Line EC and line FD are parallel. You can write this as $\overleftrightarrow{EC}$ ‖ $\overrightarrow{FD}$.

Relating Lines

Name a line that is parallel to $\overleftrightarrow{AB}$ and a line that is perpendicular to $\overleftrightarrow{AB}$.

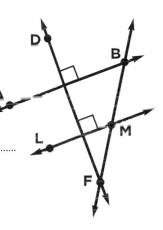

Step 1: Find a line that will never cross $\overleftrightarrow{AB}$.
$\overleftrightarrow{LM}$ will never cross $\overleftrightarrow{AB}$.
$\overleftrightarrow{LM}$ ‖ $\overrightarrow{AB}$

Step 2: Find a line that forms right angles with $\overleftrightarrow{AB}$. $\overleftrightarrow{DF}$ forms right angles with $\overleftrightarrow{AB}$.

$\overleftrightarrow{DF}$ ⊥ $\overleftrightarrow{AB}$

Lines that lie in the same plane either intersect or are parallel.

Lines that lie in different planes may intersect, be parallel, or do neither.

Lines that are in different planes and do not intersect are called **skew**.

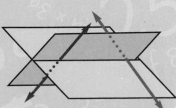

④ Angles

Angles are formed where
lines, rays, or line segments intersect.

Angles

An angle is formed by two rays that share an endpoint.
The shared endpoint is called the **vertex**.

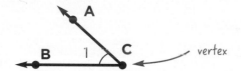

You can name an angle in three ways using the angle symbol (∠).
- Use the vertex. The angle above is ∠C.
- Use three letters in this order: a point on one ray, the vertex,
  and a point on the other ray. This is ∠ACB or ∠BCA.
- Use a number that is inside the angle. This is ∠1.

Naming Angles

Use two ways to name the angle
formed by MN and MB.

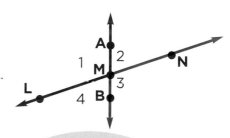

Step 1: Name the angle using
the number inside the angle.

∠**3**

Step 2: Name the angle using
a point on one ray, the vertex M,
then a point on the other ray.

∠**NMB or** ∠**BMN**

You cannot
use the name ∠M
for this angle.
There are four angles that
have a vertex at point M.

Angle Measurement

The measure of an angle tells how far one ray is turned from the other. Angles are measured in units called **degrees**. The symbol (°) means "degrees." 90° is read "ninety degrees."

| No turn at all is 0°. | A quarter turn is 90°. | A half turn is 180°. | A full turn, or a complete circle, is 360°. |

Classifying Angles

Angles are classified by how they relate to 90° and 180°.

∠1: **Acute angles** measure less than 90°.

    ∠1 is an acute angle.

∠2: **Right angles** measure exactly 90°.

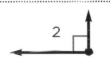

    ∠2 is a right angle.

∠3: **Obtuse angles** measure greater than 90° and less than 180°.

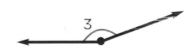

    ∠3 is an obtuse angle.

∠4: **Straight angles** measure exactly 180°.

    ∠4 is a straight angle.

∠5: **Reflex angles** measure greater than 180° and less than 360°.

    ∠5 is a reflex angle.

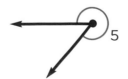

13

⑤ Angle Relationships

Some angles are related
by their positions or their measurements.
These related angles have special names.

Related Angles

adjacent angles—Angles that share a
   vertex and a side. ∠1 and ∠2 are
   adjacent angles. They share
   vertex A and side AB.

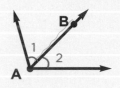

congruent angles—Angles that have the same measure.
   The word *congruent* means "the same as," or "equal."
   The symbol for congruent is ≅.

complementary angles—Two angles whose measures
   add up to 90°.

supplementary angles—Two angles whose measures
   add up to 180°.

Congruent Angles

Which angle is congruent to ∠HKM?

Step 1: Find the measure of ∠HKM. ∠HKM measures 48°.

Step 2: Find another angle that measures 48°. The measure of
∠2 is 48°. ∠HKM and ∠2 have the same angle measure, so they
are congruent.

∠2 ≅ ∠HKM

Angle Sums

Which two angles are complementary?

Step 1: The angle sum of complementary angles is 90°. To find the angle sum, add the measures of two angles. Which two angle measures add up to 90°?

The measure of ∠1 is 30°.
The measure of ∠4 is 60°.

30° + 60° = 90°

∠1 and ∠4 are complementary.

When complementary angles are adjacent, they form a right angle.

Which two angles are supplementary?

Step 1: The angle sum of supplementary angles is 180°
Which two angle measures add up to 180°?

The measure of ∠2 is 45°.   **45° + 135° = 180°**
The measure of ∠3 is 135°.

∠2 and ∠3 are supplementary.

When supplementary angles are adjacent, they form a straight angle.

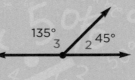

⑥ Angles of Intersecting Lines

When two lines intersect, they form four angles. The four angles are related in special ways.

Intersecting Lines

The four angles formed by two intersecting lines go all the way around the point of intersection. The sum of the measures of the four angles is 360°.

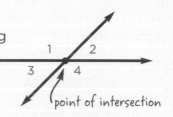

linear pair—Two adjacent angles that are formed when two lines intersect. Linear pairs always form a straight line, so they are supplementary (add up to 180°).

For the figure above, the linear pairs are:

∠1 and ∠2　　　∠2 and ∠4　　　∠3 and ∠4　　　∠1 and ∠3

 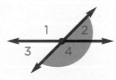  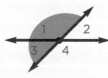

vertical angles—Two angles that are NOT next to each other when two lines intersect. Vertical angles always have the same measurement, so they are congruent.

For the figure above, the vertical angles are:

∠1 and ∠4　　　　　　　　　∠2 and ∠3

Linear Pairs

What is the measure of ∠2?

Step 1: Decide what you know from the figure.

You know: **∠1 and ∠2 are a linear pair.**
                    The measure of ∠1 is 65°.

Step 2: Linear pairs are supplementary angles.
The angle sum of supplementary angles is 180°.

       measure of ∠1 + measure of ∠2 = 180°

Step 3: Write in the angle measures that you know.

       65° + measure of ∠2 = 180°

Step 4: Subtract 65° from 180° to find the measure of ∠2.

       measure of ∠2 = 180° - 65° = 115°

The measure of ∠2 is 115°.

Vertical Angles

What is the measure of ∠3?

Step 1: Decide what you know from the figure.

You know: **∠1 and ∠3 are vertical angles.**
                    The measure of ∠1 is 65°.

Step 2: Vertical angles are congruent.
Congruent angles have the same measure.

      ∠1 and ∠3 have the same measure.
      ∠1 measures 65°, so ∠3 measures 65°.

The measure of ∠3 is 65°.

Plane figures are flat, like a shadow on a piece of paper. They are called plane figures because they lie on one plane.

Plane Figures

A **side** is a curve or line segment that is part of a plane figure.

A **vertex** is a point where line segments or curves of a figure meet. *Vertices* is plural for *vertex*.

A **closed figure** is a plane figure that begins and ends at the same point.

An **open figure** does not begin and end at the same point.

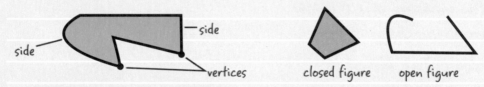

side   side   vertices   closed figure   open figure

A **polygon** is a special kind of plane figure. Polygons are closed plane figures with sides that are all line segments.

polygon   not a polygon   not a polygon   not a polygon

Regular polygons have sides that are all the same length and angles that all have the same measure.

regular   not regular   regular   not regular

Polygons

Polygons are classified by the number of sides or angles they have. Some common polygons are in the following table.

Name of Polygon	Sides	Angles	Examples
Triangle	3	3	
Quadrilateral	4	4	
Pentagon	5	5	
Hexagon	6	6	
Octagon	8	8	
Nonagon	9	9	
Decagon	10	10	
Dodecagon	12	12	

Name the shape of the following road signs.

Step 1: All of the sides are line segments that are the same length, so this is a regular polygon. Count the number of sides.   **8**

Step 2: What polygon has eight sides?

This sign is a regular octagon.

MAIN STREET

Step 1: All of the sides are line segments, but they are not all the same length. This is a polygon, but not a regular polygon. Count the number of sides.   **5**

Step 2: What polygon has five sides?

This sign is a pentagon.

19

⑧ Triangles

The prefix *tri–* means "three,"
so the word *triangle* means "three angles."
Triangles also have three sides
and three vertices.

Naming a Triangle

Triangles are named by listing the vertices of the angles in any order. The symbol for *triangle* is △.

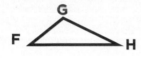

This triangle can be named △FGH, △GHF, △HFG, △HGF, △GFH, or △FHG.

The angles of a triangle always have a sum of 180°. If you tear off the corners of any triangle and put their vertices together, the angles form a straight line.

Triangle Classes

Triangles can be classified by the measure of their angles. The angles in a triangle can be acute, right, or obtuse.

Triangles can also be classified by the length of their sides. The sides can be all different, two congruent, or all congruent. A triangle with congruent sides also has congruent angles.

Small lines or hatch marks are used to show that sides or angles are congruent.

Remember, congruent means "equal."

20

Triangles Classified by Angle Measure		
Acute triangle	three acute angles	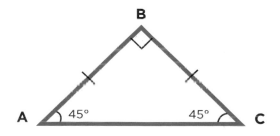
Right triangle	one right angle two acute angles	
Obtuse triangle	one obtuse angle two acute angles	
Triangles Classified by Side Length		
Scalene triangle	no equal sides	
Isosceles triangle	two equal sides	
Equilateral triangle	three equal sides	

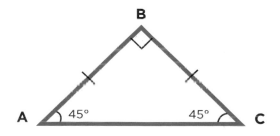

Classify △ABC by angle measure and by side length.

Step 1: Classify △ABC by the measure of its angles. There is one right angle. The other two are acute angles.

△ABC is a right triangle.

Step 2: Classify △ABC by the length of its sides. Two sides have the same length, so they are congruent.

△ABC is an isosceles triangle.

Step 3: Combine the terms to classify the triangle by both angle measure and side length.

△ABC is an isosceles right triangle.

Remember:
acute < 90°
right = 90°
obtuse > 90°

⑨ Quadrilaterals

Quad- means "four."
Lateral refers to "side." Quadrilaterals are polygons (see page 18) with four sides.

Quadrilateral Classes

Quadrilaterals are classified by how their sides are related.

A **kite** has two distinct pairs of adjacent (next to each other) sides that are congruent.

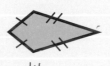

kite

A **trapezoid** has only one pair of parallel sides.

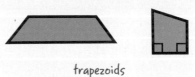

trapezoids

A **parallelogram** has two pairs of parallel sides. The parallel sides are congruent.

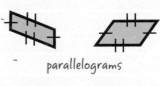

parallelograms

A **rhombus** is a parallelogram with four congruent sides.

rhombuses

A **rectangle** is a parallelogram with four right angles.

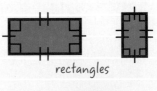

rectangles

A **square** is a rectangle with four congruent sides.

square

Overlapping Classes

Some quadrilaterals will fall into more than one class. Look at the figure and decide how many ways it can be classified.

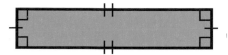

Step 1: Start at the top of the classifications on page 22. Is this figure a kite?

No, there are no adjacent sides that are congruent.

Step 2: Is this figure a trapezoid?

No, it has more than one pair of parallel sides.

Step 3: Is this figure a parallelogram?

Yes, there are two pairs of parallel sides.

Step 4: Is this figure a rhombus?

No, it does not have four congruent sides.

Step 5: Is this figure a rectangle?

Yes, it is a parallelogram with four right angles.

Step 6: Is this figure a square?

No, all four sides are not congruent.

This figure is both a parallelogram and a rectangle.

Angle Sums

The sum of the angles of a quadrilateral is always 360°. What is the measure of the missing angle?

Step 1: The corner symbol in the figure means those angles are right angles, or 90° angles. You know the measures of three of the angles. Add the angle measures that you know.

90° + 90°+ 50° = 230°

Step 2: You know the angle sum of all four angles must be 360°. You know the angle sum of three angles is 230°. Subtract to find the remaining angle measure.

360° – 230° = 130°

The missing angle measure is 130°.

⑩ Circles

Circles are not polygons.

They have no line segments.

Circles are formed by one closed curve.

Circle Terms

center—A circle is a curved set of points that are all the same distance from a given point. That point is the center.

radius—A line segment that has one endpoint on a circle and the other on the center of the circle. The plural of *radius* is *radii.*

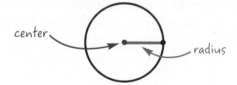

chord—A line segment that has each endpoint on the circle.

diameter—A chord that passes through the center of a circle. The diameter of a circle is always twice the radius.

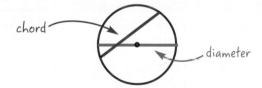

central angle—An angle formed by two radii. The vertex of a central angle is the center of the circle.

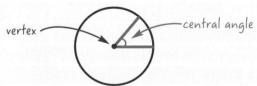

Measurements

Suppose this key ring is a circle with a radius of 15 mm. What is the diameter of the key ring?

Step 1: Diameter is twice the radius. Multiply the radius of the key ring by 2.

15 mm × 2 = 30 mm

The diameter of the key ring is 30 mm.

Semicircles and Arcs

A **semicircle** is half a circle and includes the diameter.
Semicircles are named using the two endpoints of the diameter and one other point on the half circle.
Semicircle ACB can also be called semicircle ABC, BAC, BCA, CAB, or CBA.

semicircle ACB

An **arc** is part of the curve of a circle.
A **major arc** is equal to or greater than a semicircle. Major arcs are named by three points that include the endpoints.
A **minor arc** is less than a semicircle.
Minor arcs are named by their two endpoints.

major arc YXZ

minor arc ZY

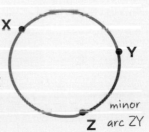

What kind of arc is the letter C?

Step 1: Look at the letter C. Is it equal to or greater than a semicircle? **Yes.**

The letter C is a major arc.

25

Prisms

In geometry, the word *solid* has a different meaning than you might usually use. Solid figures are ones that are not flat.

Solid Figures

solid figure—A geometric figure that has has three dimensions: length, width, and height.

two dimensions: not a solid

three dimensions: solid

polyhedron—A solid figure with all flat surfaces. Each flat surface is a polygon. There are no curved surfaces.

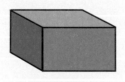

polyhedron

not a polyhedron

face—A flat surface of a solid figure.
base—The face of a solid figure that names the figure.
   Some solids have two bases.
edge—The line segment on a solid figure where two faces meet.
vertex—A corner point of a solid figure.

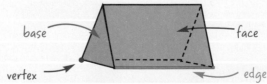

base   face

vertex   edge

Prisms

A **prism** is a polyhedron that has two congruent, parallel bases. All of the other faces are rectangles. Prisms are named by the shape of their bases. For example, a triangular prism has bases that are triangles.

triangular prism

rectangular prism

A **cube** is a square prism (has bases that are square) with faces and bases that are all congruent. All of the edges of a cube are the same length.

cube

Prism Parts

The number of faces, edges, and vertices that a prism has is determined by the shape of the bases. The table below lists a few.

Base Shape	Faces = base sides + 2	Edges = base sides x 3	Vertices = base sides x 2
Triangle	5	9	6
Pentagon	7	15	10
Octagon	10	24	16

How many edges are there on a hexagonal prism?

Step 1: The base of a hexagonal prism is a hexagon. How many sides does a hexagon have?

6

Step 2: Multiply the number of sides by 3.

6 × 3 = 18

A hexagonal prism has 18 edges.

⑫ Pyramids

Pyramids have been used in architecture since ancient times. Their shape is used to form tombs, temples, monuments, and even modern museums.

Pyramids

A **pyramid** has one base. There is a triangular face for each base side. The faces meet at a common point. Pyramids are named by the shape of their base. For example, a rectangular pyramid has a base that is a rectangle.

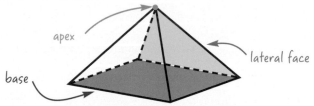

apex

lateral face

base

lateral face—A triangular face of a pyramid.
apex—The vertex where all the triangular faces meet.

Naming the Parts

Classify the pyramid and name the vertices, edges, and faces.

Step 1: Classify the pyramid by the shape of its base.
How many sides does the base have? **5**
What polygon has 5 sides?
A pentagon has 5 sides.

This is a pentagonal pyramid.

Step 2: Name the vertices.
The vertices are the corner points.

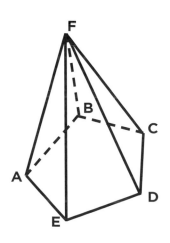

Vertices of a pyramid include the apex and the points where the base meets two faces.

The apex is point F. Other vertices are points A, B, C, D, and E.

The vertices are points A, B, C, D, E, and F.

Step 3: Name the edges.
Edges are line segments where two faces meet.

The edges are $\overline{AB}$, $\overline{BC}$, $\overline{CD}$, $\overline{DE}$, $\overline{AE}$, $\overline{AF}$, $\overline{BF}$, $\overline{CF}$, $\overline{DF}$, and $\overline{EF}$.

Step 4: Name the faces.
The base and lateral faces are all faces of a pyramid. Name each face by listing the polygon's vertices in order.

The faces are pentagon ABCDE, △ABF, △BCF, △CDF, △DEF, and △EAF.

Pyramid Parts

Like a prism, the number of faces, edges, and vertices a pyramid has is determined by the shape of the base.

Base Shape	Faces = base sides + 1	Edges = base sides x 2	Vertices = base sides + 1
Triangle	4	6	4
Quadrilateral	5	8	5
Pentagon	6	10	6
Hexagon	7	12	7
Octagon	9	16	9
Nonagon	10	18	10

Cones and cylinders are different
types of solid figures.
They do not have polygons for bases.

Cones

The base of a **cone** is one closed curve. Most cones have a base
that is a circle. A cone has an apex, a base, and one lateral face.

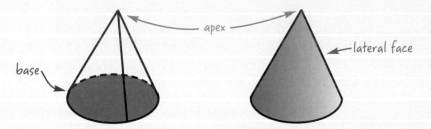

The **height** of a cone is the line segment that connects the apex
of the cone to the base at a right angle.

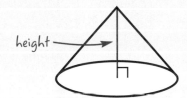

When the base is a circle and
the height is at the center
of the circle, the cone is
called a **right circular cone.**

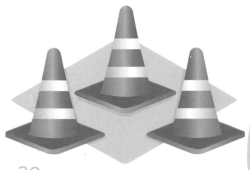

Cones are found
all over the world.
There are traffic cones, ice
cream cones, cone-shaped hats,
and volcanos and mountains
that are cone-shaped.

Cylinders

A **cylinder** is a solid with two parallel bases that are congruent
closed curves. Cans are usually shaped like cylinders. So are
paper towel rolls and most water pipes.

The **height** of a cylinder is a
segment that connects both
bases at right angles.

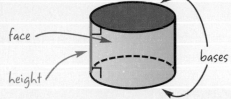

Nets

*If you cut around the bases and down the face of a solid, then
flatten them, the result is called a net. In the net of a cylinder,
what shape does the face of a cylinder make?*

Step 1: Cut around one base of a cylinder.
Fold it up.

Step 2: Cut around the second base
of a cylinder. Fold it down.

Step 3: Cut a straight line down the
face of the cylinder. Unroll the face.

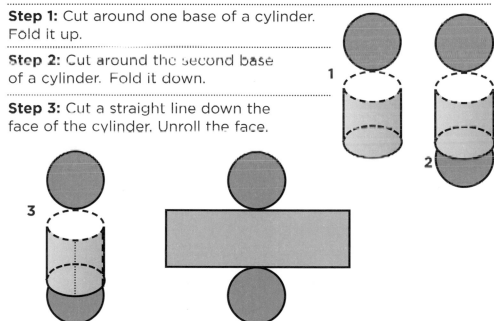

The face of a cylinder unrolls into a rectangle.

⑭ Spheres

Spheres are solid figures,
but they do not have any bases.
Earth is a sphere. So is a ball.

Spheres

A **sphere** has no bases. It is one smooth curved surface, on which every point is the same distance from the center.

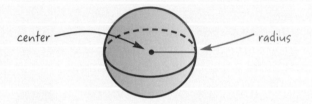

center ———→   ←——— radius

The term **sphere** is used to describe things that are round like balls. They can be solid or hollow. In geometry, a sphere is more like a soap bubble than a ball. You can measure from one side of the bubble to the other, but the thickness of the shell does not have a measurement.

Cross Sections

Imagine a plane slicing a sphere. What shape would be made at the intersection of the plane and sphere?

Step 1: Picture a plane slicing a sphere. The slice can be made anywhere across the sphere. Look at the plane figure that is made where the plane intersects the sphere.

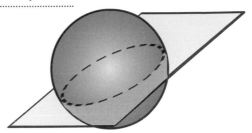

Step 2: What plane figure do you see?

The plane figure is a circle.

In a sphere, any slice is going to result in a circle. Where the slice is made determines the size of the circle.

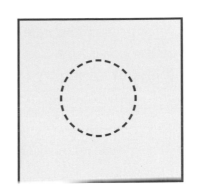

 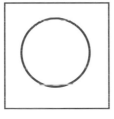  

The largest possible circle will include the center point.

Two-dimensional slices of solid figures are called **cross sections** or **plane sections**.

33

When some figures are folded
in half, the two parts will match
exactly, like mirror images.

Symmetry

A figure has **line symmetry** when one half of it is a mirror image
of the other half. Sometimes this is just called **symmetry**.
A **line of symmetry** divides a figure into two matching parts.

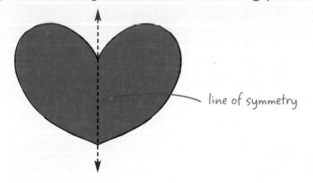

line of symmetry

Some figures have no symmetry. Others have one, two, or even
more lines of symmetry.

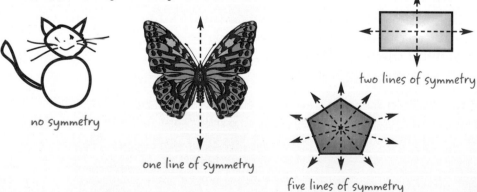

no symmetry

one line of symmetry

two lines of symmetry

five lines of symmetry

Letter Symmetry

Many numbers and capital letters have one or more lines of symmetry. In the word MATH, which letters are symmetric?

Step 1: Does the letter M have any lines of symmetry?

Yes

Step 2: Does the letter A have any lines of symmetry?

Yes

Step 3: Does the letter T have any lines of symmetry?

Yes

Step 4: Does the letter H have any lines of symmetry?

Yes.

All the letters in MATH are symmetric.

Polygon Symmetry

How many lines of symmetry are in a square?

Step 1: You can tell if a shape has a line of symmetry by making a paper model. If you can fold the model one time into two matching parts, the fold line is a line of symmetry.

Fold a square on the diagonals (from corner to corner). The two parts are matching triangles. You can make two different diagonal folds.

lines of symmetry

Step 2: Fold from the center of one side to the center of the opposite side. The parts are matching rectangles. You can do this two ways. Fold top to bottom, and side to side.

A **diagonal** is a line that connects any two nonadjacent vertices of a polygon.

There are four lines of of symmetry in a square.

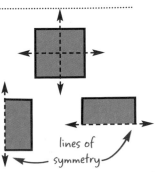

lines of symmetry

35

⑯ Congruence

If you make an exact copy
of a figure, the copy and the original
are congruent. Congruent figures are
exactly the same shape and size.

Congruent Figures

Congruent line segments have the same length.
Congruent angles have the same measure.
Congruent figures have all congruent sides and angles.
One congruent figure will fit exactly on top of the other.

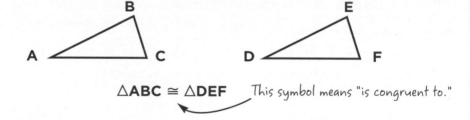

△**ABC** ≅ △**DEF**   This symbol means "is congruent to."

Comparing Figures

Are the given figures congruent?

Step 1: One way to decide if figures are congruent is to put them on top of each other. If they line up exactly, the figures are congruent.

The figures do not line up, so they are not congruent.

Correspondence

When you compare figures, the sides that match each other are called **corresponding sides**. The angles that match each other are called **corresponding angles**.

In congruent figures, corresponding sides and corresponding angles are also congruent.

Corresponding Parts

Trapezoid JKLM and trapezoid RSTU are congruent. What is the length of side ST?

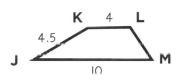

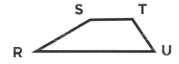

Step 1: Imagine the trapezoids lying one on top of the other. Which sides and angles correspond?

Corresponding sides:	Corresponding angles:
$\overline{JM} \cong \overline{RU}$	$\angle J \cong \angle R$
$\overline{JK} \cong \overline{RS}$	$\angle K \cong \angle S$
$\overline{KL} \cong \overline{ST}$	$\angle L \cong \angle T$
$\overline{LM} \cong \overline{TU}$	$\angle M \cong \angle U$

Step 2: Congruent sides have the same measure. The length of side ST is the same as the length of side KL. Side KL is 4 units long.

The length of side ST is 4 units.

When the problem does not tell you what the units are, use the word units rather than leave the units off.

Similar figures are alike
but not always exactly the same.

Similar Figures

Similar figures have the same shape.
They do not need to be the same size.

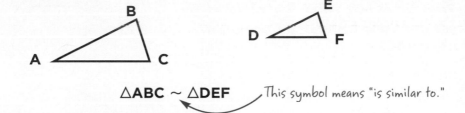

△**ABC** ~ △**DEF**   This symbol means "is similar to."

An enlargement or reduction of a picture makes a similar picture.

The shapes are the same, but the sizes are different.

Similar Figure Correspondence

Similar figures, like congruent figures, have corresponding parts.
The corresponding angles of similar figures are congruent.
The corresponding sides of similar figures are proportional.
That means the ratios of the lengths of corresponding sides
are the same.

Similar Polygons

Are △GHJ and △KLM similar?

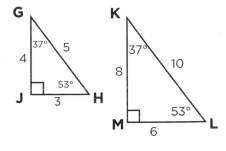

Step 1: Are the corresponding
angles congruent?

    Yes.   ∠G ≅ ∠K
              ∠H ≅ ∠L
              ∠J ≅ ∠M

Step 2: Are the corresponding sides proportional?
Write a ratio to compare each pair of corresponding sides.

$$\frac{\text{length of GH}}{\text{length of KL}} = \frac{5}{10} = \frac{1}{2}$$

$$\frac{\text{length of JH}}{\text{length of ML}} = \frac{3}{6} = \frac{1}{2}$$

The corresponding sides all
have the same ratio, 1 to 2.

$$\frac{\text{length of GJ}}{\text{length of KM}} = \frac{4}{8} = \frac{1}{2}$$

△ GHJ ~ △KLM

To check for
similarity, always check
the ratios of the sides.

Both a square and a rectangle have
four 90° angles, but that does not
make them similar figures.

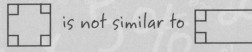

is not similar to

⑱ Slides (Translations)

When you slide a coin over a surface like a table, its shape and size stay the same. It just moves to another place. In geometry, figures can slide the same way.

Translations

In geometry, a **slide** is also called a **translation.** A translation moves each point in a figure the same direction and the same distance. The original figure and its translated image are congruent, and they face the same direction.

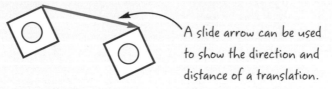

A slide arrow can be used to show the direction and distance of a translation.

Recognizing a Slide

Which set of triangles shows a slide, or translation?

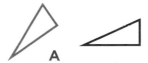
A

B

Step 1: Look at the triangles in set A. Draw a ray, called a slide arrow, from each vertex to its corresponding vertex. The slide arrows are not all the same direction or length. The slide arrows show that each vertex moved differently. The triangles do not face the same way. This is not a slide.

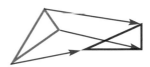

40

Step 2: Look at the triangles in set B. Draw a slide arrow from each vertex to its corresponding vertex. The slide arrows are the same direction (parallel) and the same length. The slide arrows show that each vertex moved in the same way.
The triangles face the same way.
This is a slide.

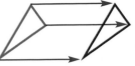

The triangles in set B show a slide, or translation.

Drawing a Slide

An easy way to slide a polygon is to use a grid. Use the grid to slide this figure three units left and five units down.

Step 1: From any vertex count three units left and five units down. Draw a new vertex at the new point. The new corresponding vertex takes the same letter name with a small line like an apostrophe (').
A' is read "A prime."

Do this for each vertex.

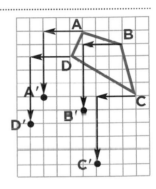

Step 2: Connect the new vertices. Since every vertex moved the same distance in the same direction, all of the sides did also.

The new figure is a translation, or slide, of the original.

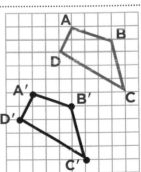

You can also use a stencil, or cutout, to show a slide. Just make sure the figures face the same direction.

41

In symmetric figures, one half of
a figure can be flipped over a line of symmetry
to match the other half (see page 34).
When a whole figure is flipped over a separate
line, it creates a reflection, like a mirror.

Reflections

In geometry, a **reflection** or **flip** creates a mirror image.
The image has the same size and shape as the original figure,
but it faces the opposite direction. Corresponding points on the
figures are the same distance from the line of reflection.

The line of reflection
is where the mirror
would be.

Recognizing a Flip

Which set of figures shows a flip, or reflection?

| A | B |

Step 1: The figures in both sets are the same size and shape.
In set A, the figures face the opposite direction.
In set B, the figures face the same direction.

The figures in set A show a reflection.

Drawing a Reflection

Draw a reflection of the figure.

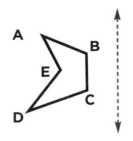

Step 1: To draw a reflection, draw a line of reflection first. The line can be horizontal, vertical, or oblique (see page 7).
Let's use a vertical line of reflection.

Step 2: From any vertex, draw a line segment that is perpendicular to the line of reflection.
Extend the line segment the same distance on the other side of the line of reflection.
Draw a new vertex.

Do this for each vertex.

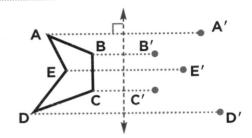

Step 3: Connect the new vertices to form a mirror image of the original figure.

A line of reflection is like a line of symmetry.
A line of symmetry splits one figure into two mirrored halves.
A line of reflection separates two mirrored figures.

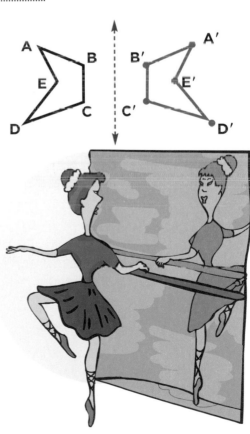

43

⑳ Turns (Rotations)

You can make a figure
face a different direction by
turning, or rotating, it.

Rotations

In geometry, a **rotation** turns a figure around a point.
The point is called the **turn center**, or **point of rotation**.
Each point on the figure turns by the same number of degrees.

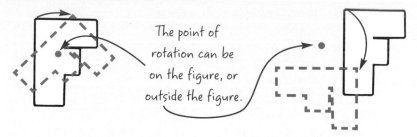

The point of
rotation can be
on the figure, or
outside the figure.

A figure can be turned clockwise or counterclockwise.

clockwise   counterclockwise

A **full rotation** is a 360° turn. A full rotation turns a figure back
to where it started. Watch what happens when you turn an
arrow clockwise 90°, 180°, 270°, and 360°.

no turn   90° turn   180° turn   270° turn   360° turn

Rotational Symmetry

Sometimes when you turn a figure, it looks the same as it did when it started, even before you make a full turn. Figures that do this have rotational symmetry. Does this figure have rotational symmetry?

Rotational symmetry is also called **turn** symmetry.

Step 1: To check for rotational symmetry, you can imagine turning the figure in your head. Or you can turn the book to see what the figure looks like when it is turned.

Try turning the figure a quarter turn (90°). Does it match the original figure? **No.**

Step 2: Try turning the figure a half turn (180°). Does it match the original figure? **Yes.** A half turn makes the image match the original figure.

Yes, the figure does have rotational symmetry.

Moving a figure to make a new figure is called a **transformation**. The new figure is called an **image**.

You can transform a figure by
1. Sliding it (a translation)
2. Flipping it (a reflection)
3. Turning it (a rotation)

Part of geometry is measurement. Some measurements are found by using a tool, like a ruler. Some measurements are found by using measurements that you already know.

Definitions

perimeter—The distance around a figure. The capital letter P is usually used to represent perimeter.

formula—A rule that is written using symbols.

Perimeter of a Polygon

Find the perimeter of this figure.

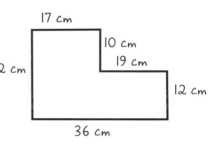

Step 1: To find the perimeter of any shape, you can add the lengths of all the sides.

17 cm + 10 cm + 19 cm + 12 cm + 36 cm + 22 cm = 116 cm

The perimeter of the figure is 116 centimeters.

To find the perimeter of something that has an unusual shape, you can use a string to measure the distance around it. Then measure the length of the string.

Perimeter of Regular Polygons

Find the perimeter of a square with a side length of 3 inches.

Step 1: A square is a regular polygon with four equal sides. You can write a formula for the perimeter of any regular polygon because you can multiply the number of sides by the length of one side.

The formula for the perimeter of a square is the number of sides (4) multiplied by the length of a side. The formula is written as:

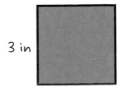

3 in

P = 4 × s, where s stands for the length of a side.

Step 2: To solve a formula, fill in the numbers that you know. You know the length of one side is 3 inches.

P = 4 × 3 inches

Step 3: Multiply.

P = 4 × 3 inches
P = 12 inches

The perimeter of the square is 12 inches.
This is the same as if you added the lengths of all the sides.
3 in + 3 in + 3 in + 3 in = 12 in

Perimeter of a Rectangle

Find the perimeter of the rectangle.

Step 1: A rectangle has opposite sides that are equal in length. The perimeter of a rectangle is 2 times the length plus 2 times the width.

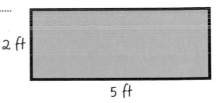

2 ft

5 ft

P = (2 × length) + (2 × width)

Step 2: Fill in the numbers you know.   **P = (2 × 2 ft) + (2 × 5 ft)**

Step 3: Multiply.   **P = (2 × 2 ft) + (2 × 5 ft)**
                                             P =   4 ft   +   10 ft

Step 4: Add.   **P = 4 ft + 10 ft**
                                             P = 14 ft

The perimeter of the rectangle is 14 feet.

47

㉒ Area: Rectangles and Squares

2a × 3a = 6a

When you decide how
much carpet, wallpaper, or paint you need
to cover something, you must find the
measurement of the area you need to cover.

Definitions

square unit—A square that is one unit long and one unit wide.
    A square inch is one inch long and one inch wide.
    You can write square units as square units, or units^2.
area—The number of square units needed to cover a figure.

Area of a Rectangle

*Aunt Millie made a quilt of squares that is 6 squares long and
4 squares wide. How many squares make up the entire quilt?*

One way: The quilt is a rectangle that
is 6 squares long and 4 squares wide.
Each square is one square unit.
You can find the area, or total number
of squares, by counting.

1	2	3	4	5	6
7	8	9	10	11	12
13	14	15	16	17	18
19	20	21	22	23	24

24 squares make up the entire quilt.

Another way: You can find the area of a
rectangle by multiplying the length times
the width. The formula is written as:

Area = length × width
$A = l × w$, or $A = lw$

Step 1: Fill in the numbers you know.

    $A = 6 × 4$

Step 2: Multiply.

    $A = 24$

24 squares make up the entire quilt.

Area of a Square

Find the area of a square with a side length of 2 inches.

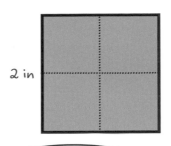

2 in

Step 1: A square has sides that are all the same length.
You can find the area of a square by multiplying a side times a side.
The formula is:

$$A = s \times s, \text{ or } A = s^2$$

This means multiply the side 2 times (side × side). It is read as "s squared" or "side squared."

Step 2: Fill in the numbers you know.

$$A = 2 \times 2, \text{ or } 2^2$$

Step 3: Multiply.

$$A = 4$$

A square with a side length of 2 inches has an area of 4 square inches.

BE CAREFUL!
A square with sides that are 2 inches long does NOT have an area of 2 square inches.

Area of a Composite

Find the area of this figure.

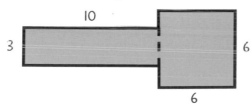

10

3

6

6

Step 1: This figure is a composite. It is a rectangle and a square that are combined. Find the area of the rectangle first.	$A = l \times w$ $A = 10 \times 3$ $A = 30$ **square units**
Step 2: Next, find the area of the square.	$A = s^2$ $A = 6^2$ $A = 36$ **square units**
Step 3: Add the areas of the rectangle and the square.	$A = 30 + 36$ $A = 66$ **square units**

The area of the figure is 66 square units.

You can use what you know
about the area of rectangles to find the
area of parallelograms.

Parallelogram Pieces

If you cut a parallelogram perpendicular to a side, you can
rearrange the pieces to form a rectangle.

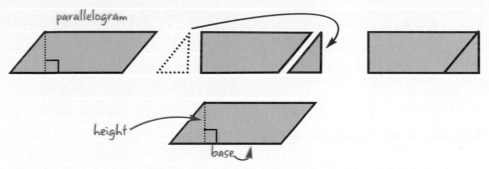

The **base** of a parallelogram can be either of the sides that
correspond to the length of a rectangle.

The **height** of a parallelogram is the length of a perpendicular
line from the base to its opposite side. The height corresponds
to the width of a rectangle.

The formula for the area of a parallelogram is similar to the
formula for rectangles.

Area of a Rectangle	Area of a Parallelogram
A = length × width	**A = base × height**
A = lw	**A = bh**

Area of a Parallelogram

Brennan is using tiles that are parallelograms to make a border design for his kitchen. Each tile has a base length of 2 inches and a height of 1.5 inches. How much area will one tile cover?

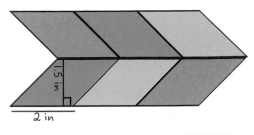

1.5 in

2 in

Step 1: Write the formula for the area of a parallelogram.

$$A = bh$$

Step 2: Fill in the numbers you know.

$$A = 2 \text{ in} \times 1.5 \text{ in}$$

Step 3: Multiply.

$$A = 3 \text{ in}^2$$

One tile will cover 3 square inches.

Remember, area is always in square units.

How many tiles will Brennan need to cover 360 square inches?

Step 1: Decide how to solve the problem. To find the number of tiles Brennan needs, you can divide the total area he needs to cover by the area of one tile.

Total area ÷ area of one tile = number of tiles needed

Step 2: Fill in the numbers you know. From the problem above, you know that each tile covers 3 square inches.

360 ÷ 3 = number of tiles needed

Step 3: Divide.   **360 ÷ 3 = 120**

Brennan needs 120 tiles.

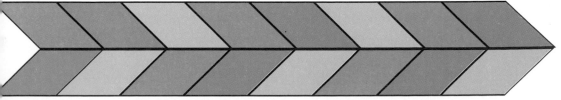

You can use what you know
about the area of a parallelogram
to find the area of a triangle.

Triangles and Parallelograms

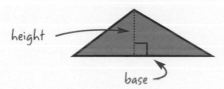

The **base** of a triangle can be any one of the sides.
The **height** of a triangle is the length of a perpendicular line
from the base to the vertex across from it.

You can take any triangle, make an exact copy of it, and form
a parallelogram. The base and height of the parallelogram are
the same as the base and height of the original triangle.

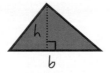 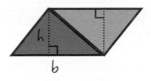

The area of one triangle is half the area of the parallelogram.

Area of a Parallelogram	Area of a Triangle
$A = base \times height$	$A = \frac{1}{2}(base \times height)$
$A = bh$	$A = \frac{1}{2}bh$

Area of a Triangle

*Ben is making a flag of Guyana
(a country in South America)
for a social studies project.
The base of the red triangle
is 12 inches. The height is 9 inches.
What is the area of the red triangle?*

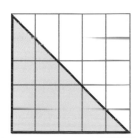

Step 1: Write the formula for the area of a triangle.　　$A = \frac{1}{2} bh$

Step 2: Fill in the numbers you know.　　$A = \frac{1}{2}(12 \times 9)$

Step 3: Multiply inside the parentheses.　　$A = \frac{1}{2}(108)$

Step 4: Multiply again.　　$A = 54$

**The area of the red triangle
is 54 square inches.**

Using a Grid

*Use a grid to count the number of units
that are covered by this triangle. Then use
the formula for the area of a triangle.
Compare the two answers.*

Step 1: Count the square units the triangle covers.

There are 10 whole units. There are 5 half units, or $2\frac{1}{2}$ whole units.

A = whole units + half units = $10 + 2\frac{1}{2} = 12\frac{1}{2}$ square units

Step 2: Use the formula.
This is a right triangle, so for
the base and height use the two
sides adjacent to the right angle.
The base is 5 units, and
the height is 5 units.

$A = \frac{1}{2} bh$

$A = \frac{1}{2}(5 \times 5)$

$A = \frac{1}{2}(25)$

$A = 12\frac{1}{2}$

Step 3: Compare the answers.

The answers are the same, $12\frac{1}{2}$ square units.

㉕ Circle Measurements

Circle measurements are a little
different than polygon measurements.
A special ratio, called pi, is used to
calculate their measurements.

Pi and Circle Formulas

Circles have their own name for perimeter: **circumference.**
The circumference of a circle is the distance around it.
In ancient times, it was found that the ratio of the circumference
of any circle to the diameter of that circle is always the
same. That ratio is represented by the Greek letter π, or **pi.**

$$\frac{c}{d} = \pi$$

Pi is an infinite decimal. That means it keeps going on and
on without ever ending or ever repeating a pattern. It is also an
irrational number. That means it cannot be written as a fraction.
In geometry, an approximate number is usually used for pi.

$$\pi \approx 3.14, \text{ or } \pi \approx \frac{22}{7}$$

This sign, $\approx$, means
"is approximately equal to."

The formula for circumference is
Circumference = π × diameter, or **$C = \pi d$**

circumference

diameter

The formula for the area of a circle is
Area = π × radius × radius, or **$A = \pi r^2$**

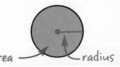

area

radius

Circumference

A swimming pool has a diameter of 28 feet. A string of decorations runs around the edge of the pool. How long is the string of decorations?

Use the value for π that makes the problem easiest to solve.

Remember, when you use an approximation for π, use the ≈ sign.

Step 1: The distance around a circle is the circumference. Write the formula for circumference.

$$C = \pi d$$

Step 2: Fill in the numbers you know.

$$C \approx \frac{22}{7}(28)$$

Step 3: Multiply.

The string of decorations is about 88 feet long.

$$C \approx \frac{22}{7} \times \frac{28}{1}$$

$$\approx \frac{22}{\underset{1}{7}} \times \frac{\overset{4}{28}}{1}$$

$$\approx 88 \text{ feet}$$

Area

A solar blanket can be used to warm the water in a pool. The blanket covers the surface of the water. What is the surface area of a pool with a 24-foot diameter?

Step 1: Write the formula for area of a circle.

$$A = \pi r^2$$

Step 2: Fill in the numbers you know. The problem tells you the diameter, but the formula uses radius. The radius is half of the diameter. Half of 24 is 12.

$$A \approx 3.14\,(12)^2$$

 diameter = 24 ft   radius = 12 ft

Step 3: Solve.

The area that needs covering is about 452.16 square feet.

$$A \approx 3.14\,(12)^2$$
$$\approx 3.14\,(12 \times 12)$$
$$\approx 3.14\,(144)$$
$$\approx 452.16$$

When you cover a box in
wrapping paper, the area that is covered
is called the surface area.

Surface Area

The **surface area** of a solid is the sum of the areas of all the faces.

Surface Area of a Prism

*Find the surface area of
this rectangular prism.*

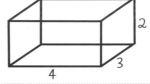

Step 1: Find the area of each face.
The bases of this prism are rectangles.
The formula for the area of a
rectangle is A = lw.

A = lw = 3 × 2 = 6 square units.

Step 2: The faces of prisms are rectangles.
Find the area of the rectangles that
appear to be on the top and bottom.

A = lw = 4 × 3 = 12 square units.

Step 3: Find the area of the rectangles
that appear to be on the front and back.

A = lw = 4 × 2 = 8 square units.

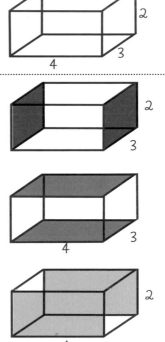

Step 4: Add the areas of all the faces.
Remember, there are two of each face.

6 + 6 + 12 + 12 + 8 + 8 = 52 square units.

The surface area of the prism is 52 square units.

Nets

A **net** is a shape that can be folded into a solid (see page 31). Use the net of a solid to help you find the surface area.

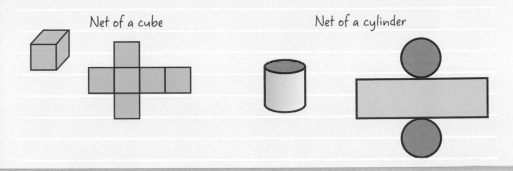

Net of a cube

Net of a cylinder

Using Nets

Use a net to find the surface area of this cube.

Step 1: Make a net of the cube. You can see that the cube is made from six squares that are all the same size.

Step 2: Find the area of one square. The formula for the area of a square is $A = s^2$.

$A = s^2 = 2^2 = 4$ **square units**

Step 3: Since each face has the same area, multiply the area of one face by 6 to find the surface area.

6 × 4 = 24 square units

The surface area of the cube is 24 square units.

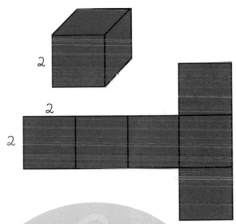

There can be more than one net for the same solid. Compare the net in this problem to the one at the top of the page. Both nets can be folded into a cube.

57

㉗ Volume: Prisms

A three-dimensional object
takes up a certain amount of space.
That space is called its volume.

Definitions

volume—The amount of space a solid figure occupies.
Volume is measured in cubic units.

cubic unit—A measure of volume that is one unit long, one unit
wide, and one unit high. A cubic inch is 1 inch long, 1 inch
wide, and 1 inch high. It can be written as 1 inch^3.

Rectangular Prisms

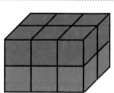

Find the volume of this rectangular prism.

Step 1: How many cubes are in
one layer of the prism?
The top layer is 3 units long and 2 units wide.
The area of the top layer is 3 × 2 , or 6 cubes.

There are 6 cubes in one layer.

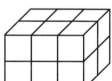

Step 2: There are two layers of cubes.
Each layer has 6 cubes in it. Multiply 2 × 6.

   2 × 6 = 12

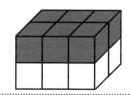

The volume of the prism is 12 cubic units.

The volume of a rectangular
prism is the area of the base
(length × width) multiplied
by the height of the prism.

*Remember:
Volume is
always measured
in cubic units.*

Formulas

The formula for the volume of a rectangular prism is:
Volume = length × width × height, or *V = lwh*
The formula for the volume of any prism is:
Volume (Prism) = Area of base × height
V = Bh
In geometric formulas, a small b is used for the length of a side, like the base of a triangle. A capital B is used for the area of a base, like the base of a prism.

Prism Volume

Find the volume of this triangular prism.

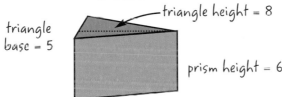

triangle base = 5

triangle height = 8

prism height = 6

Step 1: The base of the prism is a triangle. Find the area of the base using the area formula for triangles. Use *B* instead of *A* to show you are finding the area of a base.

$B = \frac{1}{2}bh$

$B = \frac{1}{2}(5 \times 8)$

$B = \frac{1}{2}(40)$

The area of the base is 20 square units.

$B = 20$

Step 2: Use the volume formula for any prism.

$V = Bh$
$V = (20 \times 6)$
$V = 120$

The volume of the prism is 120 cubic units.

The volume of a cube is easy to find. The length, width, and height are the same, so multiply the same number three times.

㉘ Volume: Cylinders and Cones

A cylinder has two congruent bases on opposite sides, like a prism. A cone tapers from the base to a single point on the opposite side.

Cylinders

The volume formulas for a cylinder and a prism are the same.

Volume (Prism or Cylinder) = Area of base × height
$$V = Bh$$

The base of a cylinder is usually a circle. The formula for the volume of a circular cylinder can be written using the formula for the area of a circle.

$$V = Bh$$
Area of base (circle) $= \pi r^2$
$$V = \pi r^2(h)$$

Volume of a Cylinder

4 cm

10 cm

Find the volume of a can that has a radius of 4 cm and a height of 10 cm.

Step 1: Use the volume formula for circular cylinders. $V = \pi r^2(h)$

Step 2: Fill in the numbers you know.

$$V \approx 3.14 \ (4)^2(10)$$

Step 3: Multiply.

The volume of the can is about 502.4 cubic centimeters.

$V \approx 3.14 \ (4)^2(10)$
$V \approx 3.14 \ (16)(10)$
$V \approx 3.14 \ (160)$
$V \approx 502.4$

Cones

A cone has one third the volume of a cylinder with the same size base. The formula for the volume of a circular cone is:

$$V = \tfrac{1}{3}\pi r^2(h)$$

Volume of a Cone

This ice cream cone has a radius of 3 cm and a height of 14 cm.
What is the volume of the ice cream cone?

Step 1: Use the volume formula for circular cones.

$$V = \tfrac{1}{3}\pi r^2(h)$$

Step 2: Fill in the numbers you know.

$$V \approx \left(\tfrac{1}{3}\right)\left(\tfrac{22}{7}\right)(3)^2(14) \approx \tfrac{1}{3} \times \tfrac{22}{7} \times \tfrac{3}{1} \times \tfrac{3}{1} \times \tfrac{14}{1}$$

Step 3: Reduce before multiplying.

$$V \approx \tfrac{1}{3} \times \tfrac{22}{7} \times \tfrac{3}{1} \times \tfrac{3}{1} \times \tfrac{14}{1}$$

$$V \approx \tfrac{1}{1} \times \tfrac{22}{7} \times \tfrac{1}{1} \times \tfrac{3}{1} \times \tfrac{14}{1}$$

$$V \approx 1 \times 22 \times 1 \times 3 \times 2$$

Step 4: Multiply.

$$V \approx 132$$

The volume of the cone is about 132 cubic centimeters.

You might see an equal sign with a dot over it ($\doteq$) instead of an equal sign with squiggly lines ($\approx$). $\doteq$ means "is nearly equal to."

Further Reading

Books

Great Source Education Group, Inc. *Math On Call.* Wilmington, Mass.:
Great Source Education Group, Inc., 2004.

Long, Lynette. *Groovy Geometry.* Hoboken: John Wiley & Sons,
Inc., 2003.

School Speciality Publishing. *The Complete Book of Algebra
and Geometry.* Grand Rapids, Mich.: American Educational
Publishers, 2005.

Internet Addresses

Banfill, J. AAA Math. "Geometry." © 2006.
<http://www.aaamath.com/geo.htm>

Math Is Fun. "Geometry." © 2007.
<http://www.mathsisfun.com/geometry>

The Math Forum. "Ask Dr. Math." © 1994–2007.
<http://mathforum.org/library/drmath/sets/mid_geom.html>

Index